Hymnal

Hymnal

Poems by

David Price-Gresty

AMELIA
Bakersfield, California

Hymnal won The Amelia Chapbook Award, 1986

The author wishes to thank the editors of *Amelia, Inscape, Ninnau, The Sandcutters, Visions* and *Wide-Open Magazine* where some of these poems first appeared.

For Veida

Cover Design: DENICE J. SZAFRAN CHONKA

First Edition
ISBN: 0-936545-08-9

"Nothing is more dreary or depressing
than the mournful drone of a Welsh choir singing in chapel
on a cold, wet, rainy Sunday morning."

James Morris

"Praise the Lord! We are a musical nation."

The Reverend Eli Jenkins
Under Milk Wood by *Dylan Thomas*

CARDIFF

I am home
in the rock of the womb
my father fled.
The taste of dirt lingers
in my mouth; perhaps
the grist of coal dust.
The stench of sulfur
fills the street. My nostrils
flare in resentment.
There is no heat in my groin,
only the growing pain of anger.
I stand in the space
my father stood. I am home
in the womb of a hard,
hard rock.

NORMAN'S ELEGY

To write an elegy tonight
I must drown my dark lamp,
brood in the blackness
of a new moon and wait
for a vision of angels that I know
does not exist. There are no laurels
or berries to crush, only seered ivy
too brittle to dangle in my thoughts.

A false start. I remember Norman
living in coarse, passionate clips
of motion. We met at Anne Cowie's
where we spent the afternoon
reading poetry with Ray Handy,
an actor from Cardiff.
That evening in the Golden Lion,
watching me tumble drunken
propositions off every woman in the pub,
Norman threatened to kill me.
"I know what you're up to, boyo,
and I won't stand for it. Listen, Yank.
Keep away from Anne." I jeered and taunted him
with fingers. I bought drinks for everyone
except him. I read poetry, sang
until dawn and invited three more women
to my room, according to witnesses
at the scene. At a banquet
a few nights later, after too many
pints of Felinfoel and lager, the evening
settling into a glaze, Norman turned to me,
smiled, lifted a glass and shouted,
"Iechyd da, Daffydd!" I ignored
him, forgot his long arm snaked across Anne's
shoulder and asked Helen to come live with me
in America. She demurely refused.

One afternoon alone in the Golden Lion,
cuddling Welshman's ruin (a pint
and a shot), waiting for my brain

to flare, Norman bought me a pint,
apologized and told me where he had been
up until now. A war, an Army hospital
in Egypt, an illness left unnamed,
the broken vows of marriage, the distance
from children, the school in the hills
where he teaches, hates the faculty
and favors the students.
He promised to loan me two books
of poetry: one by Dylan, the other
by David Jones. We sat in the dark
light of the pub, reeling
from the waltz of words like two old
dancers guiding and gliding thoughts
to a careful, slow beat. With
a grizzly wink dawned from whiskey,
Norman said, "Listen, you're a poet.
Here's something to remember . . .
We live in the last fifth
of the Twentieth Century. Drink up,
while it's still popular." When I left
Wales a few days later, I didn't see
Norman, but nestled between
the handles of my suitcase
were two books of poetry, each stamped,
"Pembrokeshire Public School Library."

Norman met his death on the coast road
walking home one night. They think
he blacked out and fell off the ledge,
smashing his skull on the rocks. It took
two days to find him.

To whom do I return these books?

Norman, I could drink the last fifth.
But I would rather fold this poem
into a paper airplane and loft it
out the kitchen window, knowing
no wind is strong enough
to land it in the lap of your grave.

THE HUM

She wakes
smiling,
alone in the large house, stretching
toward the lover she knows
is not there,
though his scent rests
on her skin, and his sweat sleeps
in her pores. She remembers
humming.
The hum of the night. The tug
in his eyes. The hum.
Her buzzing fingers traced dreams
into his shoulders. His mouth settled
like the reed of a flute
on her breast.

In her dark room
more silent
than a cat in gloves,
she holds her belly
in her hands, her eyes closed, searching
for the embryo
inside her.
This child
was made in daylight under a fierce sun
in the cool, rocking berth of a moored boat.
The child began humming. She hears
the soft click of her nails where
she gently held
the father inside her, breathing
together,
soft, sleek voices
singing between them, an open dream
humming inside each other.

The hum will keep them
together.
One day
one of them will forget
the tune. Perhaps he will.

Maybe she
will need cooler fingers.
The other
will hum alone, cutting the edges
off her world, sanding his rough stone smooth.
The noteless one
will hear the humming and
remember
the tune.

AMBER UNICORN

Lie down inside the night.
Wear your rings of amber.
A unicorn will rise from the river
to nestle against your shoulder;
its moon-glinted cone tangling
sleepward through your hair.

The river laps against the dock pilings;
a steady, undulating tongue nudges
your hips upon a ticking wave
you ride to measure a pause.
The unicorn is dreaming now;
his breath a blossoming mist
your skin drinks.

The stars smell of cinnamon.
Sparks of light brush
your fingers tingling.
His mane becomes your blanket,
the numinous curtain
you draw to sleep.

Before dawn, before the heron screams
its hollow call, you will still feel
the soft heat of amber upon your cheek,
the smooth, molten kiss
of the unicorn's cone.

REHEARSAL

She slumps on the bench,
her neck stiff
and aching. I stand
behind her, mindlessly
watching tourists
enter the East Wing
of the National Gallery,
my fingers kneading
her tensed muscles smooth
until I find
the small knot of pain
resting next to her spine.
I hold a burning thought
as my fingers gently
stretch the swollen muscle:
The Welsh
have no word for "goodbye."

The knot is tighter
than balled wire.
I cradle her head
in my left hand. My right
thumb digs below the tight bulb
and slides along her backbone.
A long cord of muscle
pulls loose.
As my fingers elude
the knot, probing
where they can soothe,
I smile.
The Welsh
have no word for "hello."

We have come to see
the Watteau exhibit.
She holds my hand
as we move among paintings
and rooms. I feel changed
as I study each canvas,
as I see what she sees;
the soft strokes
of light, the hazy
landscapes, the gentle wit
of an artist's craft.
I stand behind her,
cradling a warm bird,
holding her belly
in my hands. We are glued
tighter than spoons
asleep in a drawer.

I look beyond
savoyards, clowns and bright,
round maidens to a turnstile
at Heathrow. I see
the long corridor and the jet's
domed cockpit. I watch
her leave, knowing
the seeds of Spring grow
in her womb; like the kiss
on her thigh, blossoms
unfold in winter.

I do not regret
I have no word
for "goodbye."

REUNION

A bullfinch
budding
in a gray suit
he waits
at the railing
outside Customs
at the airport.
He has no watch
no trace of time
on his wrist.
He is not late. He waits
folding fear away
neat and matron-crisp
as a spinster's shawl and fading gloves
crease-free
as an executive's shirt.
He waits
between cigarettes
and images.
Will she part the air
with her fingers
and reach inside his chest
for warmth?
The cold, man-made
metal doors open.
Her eyes search and find him.
Tugging the sashes of an open smile
she watches her bandit
fling her weary luggage
aside. The moment
of this miracle
in unending
lightening.

GEOMETRY

Her divorce was silent.
A judge's gavel struck,
but she did not hear
the crack of wood
on wood. Across the table
her lover lights a cigarette
inhaling mute vibrations
exhaling curls of doubt.
    He wonders if his hands
    hear her skin shudder.
    Rolling her plump nipple
    between two knuckles,
    he feels
    death.
She studies the heat in his eyes.
The burnt match trembles captive
between two sliding fingers.
Her hands are empty,
no answers to the questions
between them. Why is she here?
Her fingers mesh
with a lost prayer,
then stretch to mold a peak
of a pyramid.
Her thumbs meet
and she stares into the abyss,
barely recognizing
the sides of the triangle
in her hands.

PRECEDENT

In the attic
padlocked in a cedar trunk
is a wedding gown
belonging to a grandmother
from Rouen.
The satin is worn
with streams of yellow wrinkles
like tarnished silver
placed carefully
on an old lace tablecloth.
Even held high,
snow veils of virgin dust
touch reverently to the floor.

FIRE

I met fire, and I wasn't burned.
Its fingers were softer than mine,
gentle enough to pry my hand from the gate.
I lifted the latch myself.

I met fire. I slept inside its flame
and dreamt of caves where I have hidden
a white body crouched behind coarse rocks
waiting to cringe at the first shaft of light.

I met fire. I rested on red coals
no longer needing to explode
to shatter the glass of some dark window.
I wrap my arms around the flame;
my body responds to light.

I met fire; I lit a candle outside the door.
Now, when wounded, I crawl to the hearth
seeking shelter in the gentle circle of flame.
The clean force of heat hears the echo
in my spasms, the broken phrases
I have yet to speak.

THE CULTIST

(Jonestown, Guyana; November 19, 1978)

His robe of drenched satin
swirled choirless toward the podium.
A passing hush
tumbled through the pews.
Their lips, dyed with hunger,
still tasted from
the tin cups of beggars,
praying his loose change
would drop inside:
        "Weary eyes, stop looking.
        Rest, my broken rainbows.
        My love will open you
        like a window. The air
        will flow between us."

Whispering,
blowing feathers of hope upon their eyelids,
his arms spread like wild birds
fleeing winter. He embraced them:
        "Give me your pain,
        your last aching sorrow.
        Rest, broken rainbows;
        lie down and sleep beside me."

Healing hands
swept away suffering.
Warm hands
left an ember upon their wounds.
Light hands
kneaded flesh into water.
Soft hands
molded water into wine.
Mended now, bright flames
leapt from their thirst:
        "Weary eyes, stop looking.
        Rest, my broken rainbows.

My love will open you
like a window. The air
will flow between us.
I will sing to you.
My words have been blessed
by your music.
Come; let us march
hand in hand
into death."

RUBICON

I. ROMANS

"As it is written, there is none righteous,
no, not one."

Romans 3:10

Lie down inside me.
Cool the white heat
until I am buried
in the funnel of your heart.
Forget the wild mushroom
searing the air.
There is no word for us;
we are deaf to explosions.
Do not listen to the cracking air;
some one has ripped all reason.
Darkness will settle
on the Earth's breath.
I will die
the white part
of your bones.

Einstein split the atom.
Von Braun split a puffing globe.
Alone, separate, the old, brooding eyes
lost the secret. Tucking sight under his arm,
Herr Doctor stretched his moustache
into a weeping smile, "Do you think
this will bring us Caesar?"

Caesar leads. Legions follow,
crests fallen, shields of open armor.
The thin stream between Cisalpine Gaul
and Rome is easy to cross;
only the act holds a final abhorrence.
The leader has his reason;
his destiny is full.

Hiroshima
spread open
the first flower of dust.
Nagasaki
the second sister
tasted the burnt tears.
She knew the wound
would not heal
in time.

I wait for the final hour
knowing I will not know,
for hatred takes no prisoners
and this malignant act
will leave no survivors.

Light a candle outside the door.
I have come to pray.
Close the soft-haired door.
I need to weep.
Only when I am inside you,
will there be peace in death.

Truman hung his sorrow in the closet.
He did not rend his hair.
He forgot to rip his shirt.
He stood solemnly at the guarded window
listening to a bluebird sing Genesis
to its mate. He took comfort.
He had saved the lives of our boys.

I am thankful
I leave no offspring
no bright worms
to burn in the soil.
They are spared.

Who chose this boundary,
this barely lisping stream?
Rubicon bubbled as softly as a mouse
into a narrow, green-hipped valley
that burst with pheasants

and open-mouthed meadows.
Peasant women spread their thighs
to bathe in the hot, seeping sun
their legs brown as the soil.
The men longed to taste the Earth
to smell the soil
to rest inside the warmth.
Who chose this battlefield?
Who declared war?
Who left heads bleeding in the grass?
Was the press barred?

Rome was divided.
The Senate voted.
Caesar must be stopped.
At the Rubicon.

The Ohio split North and South.
McArthur crossed the Yalu.
Caesar conquered Rome.
Hissing jets strafed Panmunjom.
Generals wept in Appomattox.

In the beginning,
we were separated by water.
Now, we are separate.

We know now
Caesar's wife was barren.
Grant stayed drunk.
McArthur obeyed a Higher Authority.
I am afraid to have children.

Caesar surveyed his troops.
The dawn hung in oblivion.
The sun dried on his hooves.
He lifted his head in drowsy dignity,
"Will you help me take Rome?"

The river waits for you.
The thin stream knows you are waiting.
Rubicon wants to act.
You are all about acting.

RUBICON

II. HEBREWS

"In burnt offerings and sacrifices . . .
thou hast had no pleasure."

Hebrews 10:6

Seeing you now
naked and open
loving and seeking
breaks what is left
of my heart.
The skin will shred from your face.
The flesh will blow away from your bones.
The fetus will shrivel in your womb.
The heart will turn to stone.
The dream will not be dreamt.

Was Eisenhower a golfing prophet
swinging his warnings of doom
and destruction bubbling in the core
of a weapon-breeding complex?
Did he foresee a hologram cowboy
riding across the firing range
on the back of a piercing missile
torn index cards bleeding
from dry, dying, smacking lips?

Who chose this river,
this thin stream
one has to stretch
to drown in?
Whoever dreamt this dream
has left us dying
at his wake.

Caesar took three years
to enter Rome.
The Kaiser tumbled in Germany in four.
The little, ugly corporal,
his ovens at full flame,
brooded and limped
for twelve raining years.

Now, we play at war.
Conventional armies
of unconventional boys
burn and strafe
Afghanistan, Chad,
Lebanon, Nicaragua,
Ethiopia, East Timor,
Angola, Burma, Namibia,
India, the Philippines,
Korea, Campuchea, Chile,
Columbia, Mozambique, Yemen,
South Africa, Sri Lanka, Ireland,
Grenada, El Salvador.
United nations at civil war.
Who's got the button?
We do.
And so do they.

Be careful when you mount me.
I don't want you
to feel my pain.
This is our last time
together. I want it
unbroken, to see
your pleased face
as you pound
through me, as my hands
push your breasts together
before the nipples enter my mouth,
before you tremble.

Caesar surveyed his troops.
Too many horses were lame.
Too many broken men
for fighting.
The long night stretched
into dawn.
"The Rubicon!
Rome is mine
for the asking."

How dare you ask?
How dare you speak?
Rumor has it, Caesar,
you lisped.

The long, black, sleek shrine
holds nothing more than names.
A guide has a numbered book
to isolate and frame the name
you ask for.
Chuck McGinnis?
Yeah, he died in VietNam.
And you walk down
past the slabs of black marble,
counting the slabs,
noting the dates
and the battles,
until you search
the column
and touch his name.
And you cry.
Because these names
these endless names
are war.
And you know
you will never
come back here
for you hate touching
death.

RUBICON

III. REVELATION

> "And the light of candle shall shine
> no more at all in thee; and the voice
> of the bridegroom and of the bride
> shall be heard no more at all in thee;
> . . . for by thy sorceries were all
> nations deceived."
>
> Revelation 18:23

You've come.
There's a pride
in helping you
get there.
This is an active voice
and we spoke together.
Now, I can rest
and build inside you.
When I decide to explode
I will create
something inside you.

Caesar scratched his balls
as he looked across
the thin river.
Crossing is easy,
he thought.
So easy,
I'll do it tomorrow.
Tonight I'll let the boys off.
Let them scrawl their names
in the Earth. Tomorrow
I'll push the button.
Tomorrow, the Armageddon.
Tomorrow, the Rubicon.

Kennedy misled and missed October.
Tet offensively goosed Johnson from office.
Nixon colored Cambodia Agent Orange.
CBS News ended the war.
Peter Kalisher flushed out Kissinger

in Paris. The rest
is peace in hand.
Howdy, hologram cowboy.
Been flicking your tongue
on the button lately?

Hail, Caesar!
The last thing
we will do
is bury you.
We are close
for comfort.
There's a joy
in watching you go off.

The button.
Who's got the button?
Or is it a lever?
Do you simply
punch buttons
on the phone?
How are you
going to end us?
Has anyone found justice
by asking questions? In California,
there is the right to die.

We are gliding now.
The heat of you
echoes in my pores.
The pleased smile you slide
down to me yanks me
into you. I hope
you taste
my soft answer
to your core.
My gentle whore,
my cool answer,
my billowed flame,
you plunge into me.
I forgot how to speak.
I answer.
I explode.
The fierce clutch
and gentle clench
are all that
we have left.

SONOGRAM

The doctor weaves the scanner
across her budding belly
and, unfolding in wisps of gray
shadow on the screen,
the ribcage of a bird,
its fierce heart billowing,
flutters in her womb.
Human limbs like wings
stretch and lope skyward
soaring over Dinas Head
above Cardigan Bay and the Irish Sea
inland past Pentra Ifan
and the crumbled, tumbled rock
of Carn Ingli to a grove
where Druids still breathe.
I stand before the Celtic Cross
and hear ancient chanting,
the bleating of the dead.
In a hallowed grove
haunted by cowled herons,
hawk-circling gulls, curlews,
magpie and rook,
I hold a small bird
in my hands I cannot offer
to these Welsh gods. I no longer
live in this land. My prayer
to the ringed cross is that
this bird perch on the stone limbs,
rain-pitted and coarse-grained,
and sing its own song.

This ageless afternoon
I stand fallow
watching the dog
race and scatter birds
and snuffle through the dry husks
of brittle, ambered leaves.
The sun glints through
stripped, skeleton-fingered trees.

A bird
unknown to me
a green cardinal
red-tufted and -tailed
glued sideways
to the dry stalk of a reed
sings in a foreign tongue.
The earth is a sponge
absorbing unfurling fury.
I barely hear the muffle
seep inside my shoes,
quickening ears alert
to a roaring, chaotic awakening.

A TOAST TO MY PEERS

Dearly beloved,
we are gathered here today
to bid good riddance
to the Revolution.
We have entered
that withered stage
we thought television,
chemicals and medical science
could forestall forever:
middle age.
Let us bear witness
to the texture of paradox:
the body's circumference
expands and shifts;
possibilities close shut;
options lose fingers.
The moon is not so mystic
when it wanes.
So, as relics of the Revolution,
let us raise our glasses of Perrier,
while there's still enough light
to jog through the park.

ON THE UNIVERSITY QUARTERBACK

Sinews snapped; bone cracked.
In the transition from motion to pain, he stopped running
on the last Saturday of October. What was once beauty
(a shard of light is only seen) now instills
muted rage, muffled in the silent groans
of a limping grace. By November they had hidden his arm
in a metal cylinder.

At parties, he staggered under tables
or sat on the pot in the ladies' restroom and lectured
on the warmth of mental inebriety. He'd take off his clothes
and cling to the nearest body. He'd hang with his arms
around our necks and ask if we believed in animated nudity.
By twelve he would be crying.

On New Year's Eve, his wife tried to hold him.
He threw out his arms, swatting, as if to protect himself,
and knocked her across the room.
Then he leaped at her . . .

He must have touched something voidless,
because when he landed he lay silent and trembling.
He lifted his head and tried to look through her.
Failing, he asked her (in drowsy dignity):
"Why was our priest bowlegged?"
She slept with him on the floor that night.

I saw him in the drugstore last March.
He threw his arms across my shoulders and whispered
(in a boozer's bellow): "Do you believe
in naive imagery? My wife thinks she's a cherub;
I think she's a male with a hole in the middle . . .
only now her navel's bloated. She wants me
to be a lawyer. I've just recovered from a mental hernia!
For a while, I thought of nothing but my alcoholic
foot. Do you remember the Wake Forest game?"

I smiled. He grabbed me
by my collar and pulled me to his face.

With the eyes of a mad dog, he raged:
"We're just females . . . with extensions."
Then he hugged me
and staggered out the door.
I ran after him and shouted: "You were
a goddamn lousy quarterback!" He turned and smiled
vaguely, leaving a faint, cascading
trace of sobriety.

NEWPORT, DYFED, WEST WALES, 5 a.m.

Tomorrow I may be sober
if the Golden Lion stays closed
if I fall asleep here
on the cobbled bulkhead
and drift on the same wave
the moored boats tilt and ride
if I leave enough stars uncounted
if the night remains this black
and unrelenting, this cold
while I fume in a drunken fire
if midtide laps and lulls me to sleep
suspended in the long link of stars
blazing cold and wet and brilliant
if the dogs I've met walking
lead the way home past
the one traffic light
that never changes
if I can freeze my life
in the clarity of this moment
then tomorrow I may be sober.

MARTIN FINSEN

As a lover,
he often had sand in his eyes.
Gravel beads hung from the lashes.
Red razor lines rimmed his pupils
with the opulent strings of a nightmare.

Martin considered himself tender
as careful as
mounds of dead snow
slipping away from the sun.

His women inevitably rankled.
Their thighs withered under his hand.
Dry lips stiffened into leather
leading to sandpaper inside.

He always granted freedom
to each layer of receding skin
for he knew of no one
more immediate than himself.

TELYN BREGUS

(Welsh: Broken Harp)

The harp needs mending;
its soft strings bent
in a brooding tangle.
If the woman's hands are noteless,
the Welshman's song is harsh,
sung for dry voices.
All my lovers are older;
all promises broken
by stirrings of remorse.
Each voice sings with one less octave.
The harp needs mending;
    I sing alone.

NOS DA

(Welsh: Goodnight)

They were already married
by the first deep blink
of winter. The holding
of each other fell snug
in the fluffed, feather-
pillowed hug of night.
Two downy birds,
that caroled, pecked,
nest-snagged and egg-stuffed,
fluttered at the edge
of the shadowy rim
of the candle's bawdy
glow. The heat turned low
on purpose; searching,
settling for sticky, not
yielding to her open bending,
he taught his skin to lie,
his eyes to thank night
for the curtain, the fierce
fumbling inside another
direction. He waited
for her trust to falter
before he said,
"Goodnight, love."

THE REVENANT

As a boy, I often wondered
why he did not live in a thatched cottage
with white walls and blue-gray shutters
or a boathouse on the Eastern Shore
with nets slung from brooding rafters.
Instead he lived in a garage
on the other side of the alley.
Dead oil splashed my nostrils.
Dust hung from the pegboard walls.
I knew his back had once been straight
and he had been a mechanic
before a cough set off cinders
caving in his chest.
In the afternoon I would find him
frozen on a box
carving ducks and alligators from soap bars
for me to launch in the bathtub
when I was alone.

I asked several times
why he did not live inside
the house with his daughter.
Each time the cough banged through his body
forcing his eyes to drip
as he rasped,
"She grieves with shame."
She watched from the kitchen window,
her fox-like fingers dug into the drapes.
He said her eyes warmed his neck.

Late in October
as the wind grew crisp enough
to sting the eyes,
he said he would move away.
He wanted to live in a boarding house in Cincinnati
where the River seemed forever swollen and black.
I thought he should live in Florida
with other old people.
His face grew dark as purple ash

as the cough slowly grew inside
ripping through his throat.
He bent and rolled like a dying bear,
his eyes brighter than glass. I ran home.

The box, through petrified,
remained visible from my kitchen window.
Not all visions end in silence.
More stoic
some slide in despair.

SOUTH GLAMORGAN BLUES

This is for the Welsh in you:
somewhere in the pit of the mountain
above Cardiff your heart
was stitched to your groin.
A slim vein of coal dust
rims your eyes
filtering light through a prism
leaving the glint of a rainbow
forever in your line of sight.
The morning still sings to you;
open notes blow through your beard.
The rich lilt of morning
pries your breastbone,
airing your heart in the dry swing
of the wind off the Severn.

This is for the clear pool of rage
still tumbling through your eyes:
your dream extends beyond light
past the broken shadows the mountain
casts through the valley.
Though your fingers will never dig
in the black dirt and touch fire,
your life is soaked in passion;
deathly silence is not your name.

DOWNPAYMENT

Foliage stutters from the cracks
in the concrete cliff
ants climb
before they crawl
under the stripping of the kitchen door.
The linoleum reeks of food stains
and crumbling dog hair.
Brown creases of a rusty stream
have bleached
the porcelain of the sink.
Layers of paint slip at random
uncovering patches of a rancid wall.
Although barely morning,
the sun hastily abandons
the room
of a house
someone like me
can not afford
to buy.

SLEEPWALKER

He roams the long
acres of woods counting shadows
of thin trees thinking
of lips as sensuous as fingers
amazed by how slender
strength is. The moon spills
its milk between the wet blades
of warm grass. The soles
of his boots slurp and squeak,
the leather wet with light.
He turns and sees the shadows
his footprints wedged
in the sponged earth.
He is a stranger
to the moon and the lost
yearning in his still-moving feet.

THE WIZARD

"I have lived several years,"
he said, "The wind has lisped
past my chair
and repeated little. I have heard
the crust break and flake
from the iron gate. Dust never
settles, but explodes
leaving silk chords
warped on the kitchen sideboard.
My sires knew much less than I;
my offspring that much more."

His hand drew tiny circles in the air
waving to the stove.
The kettle sent boiling swarms of steam
upward, clinging to the onion-skinned window.
I poured his cup of tea
and returned to the rotting cot
where he rested. His face perched
on the rim, sucking the steam into his nostrils:

"I barely felt her leave my bed.
The call she answered only spoke to her;
I heard the break in the wave.
She disintegrated slowly.
First, wanting only salt;
in the end, begging for seaweed.
She became a slave.
The sailor's whore."

Frowning, as if his veins were drenched
with smoke, he said,
"She paid me for her sin."
His eyes closed and, as I spread the ragged blanket
over him, I shivered
remembering how the watermarks mottled
her once fair skin.

BACK RIVER INLET

Tinsel willows swell
and shimmer against
the rusted surface of the shoal.
The long boughs ache
from breathing the heavy
August air. A girl's feet
turn brown from wading
as she slides silently
toward the minnow-hunting
crane. Her fingers
part the reeds and rushes
with the skilled
persistence of a knife.
Reeds don't rustle;
they whisper. Her feet move
without her. Her toes search
black, metallic mud
for broken glass and rusted cans.
She is close enough to hear
the crane's breathing, to ask
its name, to see its swimming
food float to the surface
before the sleek, white neck
darts underwater.
If she touches another
reed, the crane will stretch
its wings and lope
skyward. She doesn't
move. She trusts herself.
Today she is a silent,
gentle hunter.

TY COFFA

(Welsh: Memory's House)

In Coffa's house,
the sun is a magician
who leaps from room to room
with the grace
of a magnificent, furry cat.

In Coffa's house,
the moon rides a white stallion
across the front lawn.
She bolts from the saddle,
swaggers across the porch
and offers her business card.
"When you call Heaven," she says,
"Don't forget to reverse the charges.
The stars are family;
the brightest are the last to die:
one grandfather, one uncle,
and soon another grandmother."

On muggy days
when the skin is too wet to breathe
an invisible river
flows down the hallway
the twigs and hearts of flowers drifting
too brittle to burst in sunlight.

Now I live elsewhere
conscious of my own brittleness.
My rooms are full of functions;
my time spent with tasks.
Only my sleep is gentler
for I have strung kites
across the ceiling above my bed.

TYLWYTH
(Welsh: Family)

Grandad Price died of kidney disease
when Mam was four. Grandad Gresty
died in his sleep within a month
of our arrival in America.
I was four, then. Twice,
in my eighth and tenth summers,
Mam took us home. Dad stayed behind
both to work and to keep his distance.
We stayed with Granmam Price,
only visiting Granmam Gresty
on the now and then.
Both are dead, now; each passing
so evenly spaced that the pain
is untraceable. Four roots
were lost in this planting.
Even their names
have vanished, for no tombstones
exist in this new graveyard.
So, for Sarah Evelyn Felstead and William Henry Price,
and for Mary Elizabeth Percival and Albert Edward Gresty,
I bury a prayer for unleavened dreams
in the layers of this inconsequential poem.

BY-LINE

Well that I have aged this way
complacent
partially bleached
like the lacquer
sprayed on wicker tables
I crackle slightly
at the touch
of other fingers
stiff
though the fiber was born
flexing rigid
more amiable to bending.

THE RAINBOW FACTOR

Her last mark in the "diddle-um" club went home,
his five bob checked on the blue card
Granmam neatly snuffed into her purse.
The electric toaster he chanced
snapped shut with her smile.
She trusted the money she made off his whim.
As my Mam served tea to silent china,
Granmam proffered a theory:

> "The trouble with Welshmen
> is the coal. They've got
> grist in their eyes.
> So, when they walk
> from the pit
> to the sunlight,
> their vision's obstructed.
> They see rainbows.
> And they believe that's life.
> Never do business on a rainy day.
> Murders happen then;
> drunkenness and wife-beating.
> No one can see the rainbow."

And only Granmam noticed that the mark left his umbrella.

THE SAFE WAY

the wheels of my shopping cart
squeak
the chain-link cage bloated
with Nine Lives cat food
and a twenty-five pound
bag of Glamour
Kitty litter
the blonde in front of me
reads PEOPLE magazine
her ass mashed
in designer jeans
all roundness
flat and forgotten
I know now that I am
a symbolic Welshman
cut
from a silhouette
I live in a land that has
no wenches
no bonnie lasses
no shepherds
no pearls

my legends and lies
have been decoded
and priced by
the optical scanner
at the checkout counter

it no longer matters
that King Arthur and his knights
are hiding in the caves
of Mount Snowdonia
or that I'll never carve
my lover a spoon

they raise Welsh
palominos in California
on diets of avocado
and wine

a bill
is pending in Congress
proclaiming
Saint David the patron saint
of the Jews

I am the victim
of my own perversity
I am a self
beyond conception

Safeway
has my number
the optical scanner
blinks twice
while
the register flashes
my
Universal Product Code.

R.S.V.P.

I won't
dance at your wedding.
I won't
shake hands with the groom.
In fact,
I won't attend.
I will most likely
be in my native country
drunk and randy
in a pub.
This slim sheath
of sister-like
friendship you hand to me
now
is rejected.
You are
my oldest lover.
Your hands
once traced willows
along a river weaving
branches around my neck.
Why should I replace magic
with cordial distance?
How could you
possibly
be my friend?

MARCHOG
(Welsh: Rider)

The rider
digs his heels
into the colt's clean
flanks. The gash
goes unnoticed; only
the destination
is in sight.
The colt's pain
throttled,
its ripped skin
exchanged for a gallop.

The rider
races the open wound
home; the memory
of an unscarred colt
forever erased
by his purpose,
its possibility
only an indentation
in time.

MERASGWYN
(Welsh: Marrowbone)

He is only bone and marrow
feathers and shafts of light.
He stumbles nightly
in the finely-felt and velvet distance
between whore and home.
He preens before stones.
He dances with shadows
in the lane, his loose limbs
elongated, matching lengths
with the vines and branches
stretched taut in the dark and light.
He fumbles with the keys to his lover.
He mumbles the wrong name.
Her leg snaps the numb arrogance in his smile.
He tumbles down the stairs.
The keys crumble in his hand.

Outside a sharp crease of light
slashes a clearing in his tangled fog.
He stands straight for the first time.
Then, he tosses his bones and feathers
at the black half of the moon
leaving lunar spots to dazzle
the telescopes of the night.

HARTNETT HALL: March 21, 1972*

Just something
a faded sheet
graffiti on a vacant wall
so you'll know
I've lived here
meaningless
but appropriate
for the setting
trivia
for a scholar's thesis
when I am an artist
and thoughts
need my name:
I fear the children
will freeze me
a forgotten icicle
thawing beneath a window
(a shard of light unseen)
My fire doused, younger feet
kick the ashes
the cold, wet ashes
of a previous camper
who made the trip
without me
childlike, frozen priest
with verses of twisted music
transparent babble
liquid
in a father's breast.

*Hartnett Hall was a boarding house complex near DuPont Circle in Washington, D.C.

WEST WALES WINTER NIGHT

The wind leaps off the mountain ledge,
a hungry rook with ice on its breath,
and rumbles down the hillside,
chill-scalded talons slashing skin and fur,
before it tumbles through the cracks
in the onion-skinned windows
of the barroom in the Golden Lion.
Drinkers huddle in booths
or rub shoulders as they stand
and pass pints across the bar,
though bitter and ale are not as wanted
tonight as whiskey and malt.
The fireplace stove snaps and spits
wooden sparks and rainbowed spots,
the captured audience wrapped
like a scarf around iron and glass.

Gareth unbuttons his sweater to model
the new tee shirt mailed from Washington, D.C.
Two fried eggs cover his nipples;
the slogan circles his navel
and smiles, "sunny side up."
John Denley puts one in for Glynn.
Helen does the same for Penny.
Our Jeff sits in his usual corner
nursing a pint can of Felinfoel
his speech hushed as whispered thunder
Only a few have heard from the Yank.

The wind bites Glynn's shoulder.
He grunts at his whiskey, "Where's your quick heat?"
British Dick, commodore of the boat club,
spreads his worries across the bar top
for Glynn to finger and to poke the ashes:
Will the moorings hold
if this winter's as harsh as the last?
How much silt will settle in the Harbour?

The slow night glows like a candle in a corner.
The heat of the village is stored in this room.
Long past closing time,
after one by huddled one has trundled home,
this room will sleep cozed and warm,
while a poet in America
lays down his pen, and looks out
the kitchen window at the dull night
where the stars are not as stark
or as bright or as countless
as the ones over Newport Harbour.

DAVID PRICE-GRESTY is the Foreign Affairs and National Defense Editor for the Congressional Research Service of the U.S. Library of Congress. The former reporter and actor has written ten plays, including *Strings* and *Free Fall. The Blue Funk* was one of four finalists in the 1986 Siena College Playwriting Competition. The play will receive a staged reading at the American New Theatre in Los Angeles Next year. *Project Liberty*, a one-act play commissioned by ARTS DC, opened at the John F. Kennedy Center in April 1987 and went on tour in May. *The Rainbow Factor* won the University of Wisconsin's 1987 Playwriting Competition. The competition was judged by Playwright Israel Horovitz and drama critic Julius Novick of the *Village Voice. The Rainbow Factor*, which explores his parents' decision to emigrate from Wales in 1948, received a staged reading by the University's Dramatic Arts Department in October 1987. Four of his plays have been produced by the Source Theatre Company. His awards include the H.P. Jones Memorial Award for Creative Writing in Prose; First and Second Prizes, plus First Honorable Mention, in the 1983 Arizona State Poetry Festival; First Prize in the 1984 Amelia Awards; First and Second Prizes in the 1985 Amelia Awards; Second Prize in the 1985 Charles William Duke Long-Poem Awards; Second Prize and First Honorable Mention in the 1986 Amelia Awards, Second Prize in the 1986 Bourgoyne Awards; First Runner-up in the 1986 Wide Open Magazine Poetry Contest; First Honorable Mention in the 1987 Amelia Awards; Second Prize in the 1988 Amelia Awards; and First Prize in the 1987 Amelia Chapbook Award. He lives in Washington, D.C., with his beloved wife and certified, prize-winning muse, Veida Dehmlow, and their "toy" yellow Labrador, Spats. Their first child, Hannah Louise, was born on April 27, 1987.